D0870876

1. A column of PzKpfw IIs and PzKpfw 38(t)s of the 7th Panzer Division fights its way into Lithuania, 22 June 1941.

TANKS ILLUSTRATED No 16

Operation Barbarossa

STEVEN J. ZALOGA AND
JAMES GRANDSEN

ARMS AND ARMOUR PRESS

Introduction

Published in 1985 by Arms and Armour Press
2-6 Hampstead High Street, London NW3 1QQ.

Distributed in the United States by
Sterling Publishing Co. Inc., 2 Park Avenue,
New York, N.Y. 10016.

© Arms and Armour Press Limited, 1985
All rights reserved. No part of this publication may
be reproduced, stored in a retrieval system, or
transmitted in any form by any means electrical,
mechanical or otherwise, without first seeking the
written permission of the copyright owner.

British Library Cataloguing in Publication Data:
Zaloga, Steven J.
Operation Barbarossa. – (Tanks illustrated; no. 16)
1. Armored vehicles, Military – Germany
– History   2. Armored vehicles, Military –
Soviet Union – History
I. Title   II. Grandsen, James   III. Series
623.74′75′0943   UG446.5
ISBN 0-85368-702-1

Editing, design and artwork by Roger Chesneau.
Typeset by Typesetters (Birmingham) Limited.
Printed and bound in Italy.
by Tipolitografia G. Canale & C. S.p.A. - Turin
in association with Keats European Ltd.

The German invasion of the Soviet Union on 22 June 1941 initiated the largest tank battles the world had ever seen, but what is most striking about these battles is the disparity in forces of the opposing sides, and the one-sided victory that ensued. The Red Army in 1941 could field 24,000 tanks and 4,800 armoured cars; against these the Germans deployed 3,350 of their 5,460 tanks, plus the small tank forces from Finland, Hungary, Slovakia and Romania. Even though the German forces were substantially outnumbered, the much larger Russian force was virtually annihilated, and after three months of fighting the Wehrmacht stood poised at the outskirts of Leningrad and Moscow.

The German successes in 1941 were the result of the superior training and leadership of the panzer forces, and not to any technical advantage. German light tanks of the period, for example the PzKpfw I or PzKpfw II, did not compare favourably to the BT series or the T-26, whilst German medium tanks, such as the PzKpfw III and PzKpfw IV, were in many ways inferior to the new Soviet T-34 medium tank or the KV. Although the numbers of new Soviet tanks were relatively small, the 967 T-34s and 508 KVs made up a substantial force by German standards.

The Soviet failure in the summer of 1941 occurred in spite of important equipment and technical advantages. First, Soviet military leadership was of dismal quality. Most of the finest armoured force commanders had been shot during the purges of 1938–41, and the general officers remaining were often of poor quality. Several of the mechanized corps commanders had earlier been sacked for their scandalously poor performance in Finland in 1940, but the Red Army was so desperate for general officers that they were reinstated and, in some cases, promoted to take command of the mechanized corps. Leadership problems likewise extended into the lower officer ranks. Second, Soviet armoured force training was poor compared to German training, as with so large a tank force the Russians simply could not afford to give their crews much more than a few hundred miles of running time in their tanks each summer. The small percentage of tank crews that took part in the major summer manoeuvres usually participated in a grand form of martial choreography to impress top party officials rather than a vigorous and unpredictable tactical exercise. Third, the Soviet tank force, although large, was in a dismal state owing to the almost complete absence of spare parts. Although much of the equipment was no older than the Germans', it had not been properly supported by repair and overhaul and over half the Soviet tanks were on the verge of mechanical collapse when the war broke out. The results of these disparities are very evident throughout the following pages. If the extensive selection of photographs of burning Russian tanks seems one-sided, this is an unfortunate reminder of the outcome of that campaign.

The illustrations in this book are from the captured German photograph collection of the US National Archives, a collection unique among the Second World War German photographic archives in that much of it is captioned, with accurate unit identifications, places and dates. One of the more remarkable portions of the collection is a file of over 1,000 photos taken by photographers attached to Panzer Regiment 25, 7th Panzer Division, during the bloody battles on 22–23 June for the Nieman bridges against the Soviet 5th Tank Division; seldom has a single tank action been so amply covered, and a large number of these illustrations have been reproduced here.

Unless otherwise noted, all photos appearing here are from the RG242 collection of the US National Archives, but the authors would like to thank Esa Muikku, George Balin and Ivan Bajtos for their help in locating other photographs used in this book.

Steven Zaloga and James Grandsen

◀2
2. A rear view of a T-34 Model 1940 disabled during the fighting for Wilno on 25 June.

▲ 3

▲ 4   ▼ 5

3. On 22 June 1941, 18th Panzer Brigade entered the Soviet Union by means of an underwater crossing of the Bug river near Patulin using specially modified PzKpfw III als Tauch-panzer tanks. Here, one of the brigade's tanks makes it to Soviet soil.

4. An SdKfz 222 light armoured car and lorries of the 7th Panzer Division await orders to move forward in the fields outside Olita, Lithuania, on 22 June 1941.

5. Tanks of Panzer Regiment 25, 7th Panzer Division, form a defensive laager while refuelling on the outskirts of Olita, Lithuania, 22 June 1941. This regiment was equipped primarily with Czech-manufactured PzKpfw 38(t) tanks.

6. A mine-damaged PzKpfw 38(t) waits by the roadside outside Olita while motorized infantry passes by.

7. A Komsomolets armoured artillery tractor lies abandoned outside Olita on 22 June. This small vehicle was designed to tow light weapons like the 45mm anti-tank gun or the 76mm regimental gun; judging by its caisson, this particular vehicle was probably towing a 76mm regimental gun.

▲8　▼9

8. Although impressive in size, the Soviet T-28 medium tank was neither well armoured nor particularly well armed. This T-28 of the 5th Tank Division was knocked out by Panzer Regiment 25 west of Olita on 22 June.

9. A disabled Komintern artillery tractor. The Komintern was based on the T-12 tank chassis, and there were 1,017 in service in 1941.

10. A PzKpfw IV Ausf E of Panzer Regiment 25 knocked out during the fighting near Olita on 23 June with the 5th Tank Division.

11. Although not in service in large numbers in June 1941, the 50mm Pak 38 was the only German anti-tank gun which had even a chance of disabling one of the new T-34s if it could ambush it from the side. Here, a gun belonging to the 7th Panzer Division is towed by a Demag D7 halftrack on the opening day of the fighting near Olita.

▲12

12. A BT-7 of the 5th Tank Division after the tank battles of 22 June. The large white cross insignia just visible on the turret roof had been used during the 1940 Soviet invasion of Lithuania as an air recognition marking.

▼13

13. A T-28 Model 1934 knocked out at Olita by the 5th Tank Division on 22 June. This view clearly shows the two small machine gun turrets fitted to this vehicle, an archaic layout which, together with the vehicle's thin armour, gave little comfort to its crews.

14. Another view of the same T-28. There were about 500 of these tanks still in service in 1941.

15. A front view of the disabled T-28. The armour on this tank was only 30mm at maximum, making it vulnerable to weapons like the PzKpfw 38(t)'s 37mm gun.

16. A PzKpfw 38(t) Ausf E of Panzer Regiment 25 during the fighting at Olita on 22 June.
17. A column of PzKpfw 38(t) Ausf Es of Panzer Regiment 25 during the fighting for the Nieman bridge on 22 June.
18. The crew of an SdKfz 251 Ausf B try to move their vehicle from marshy ground near Kalvarija, 22 June 1941.
19. An SdKfz 251 serving, unusually, as an artillery tractor for a 10.5cm field howitzer. On either side are a PzKpfw III and a PzKpfw IV of the 7th Panzer Division.

16▶

▼17

18▲   19▼

▲20 ▼21

20. A PzKpfw 38(t) Ausf E of Panzer Regiment 25. Some of the tanks of this unit, like the example shown, had stowage boxes added to the turret sides.

21. Two PzKpfw IIIs pass by the remains of a PzKpfw 38(t) which had its turret blown off in the fighting for the Nieman river bridges on 22 June.

22. A PzKpfw II of Panzer Regiment 25. Although the 20mm gun of this vehicle did not compare in performance with the 45mm gun used on the BT or T-26, it was still more than adequate to penetrate the thin armour of these Soviet tanks at normal battle ranges.

23. A PzKpfw II, showing the rarely fitted anti-aircraft mounting for the MG 34 machine-gun.

22▲   23▼

▲24

▲25　▼26

24. PzKpfw IIIs of Panzer Regiment 25 pass a PzKpfw 38(t) Ausf E with its turret blown off.

25. Another victim of Russian tanks during the fighting for the Nieman river bridges was this PzKpfw II Flamm flamethrower tank which apparently suffered an internal explosion that removed its turret.

26. A BT-8 knocked out by German tanks during the initial fighting in the USSR. The white band marking around the turret roof is unusual; the turret numbering was similarly uncommon on Russian tanks.

27. A BT-8 knocked out during the fighting for the Nieman bridges. Ironically, in spite of the heroic defence of the bridges by the 5th Tank Division, the 7th Panzer Division captured them intact after Russian engineer troops failed to detonate scuttling charges.

28. A Komsomolets of the 5th Tank Division, knocked out south of Kalvarija on 22 June; a PzKpfw II Flamm can be seen in the background.

▲29 ▼30

29. German troops inspect a BA-20 light armoured car knocked out near Terebekji on 22 June. This vehicle was the standard light scout of the Soviet Army.

30. A BT-7 Model 1935 and a BT-7 Model 1937 near Samnykai, Lithuania, 26 June 1941. Note that the Model 1935 still has the 1940 invasion cross on the roof.

31. A BT-5 Model 1934 fast tank knocked out near Samnykai on 26 June. The BT-7 Model 1935 employed the same turret as the BT-5 Model 1934 and so is often mistaken for the latter; however, the Model 1935 featured a re-designed hull.

32. A T-26S Model 1939 abandoned in a river near Lumma on 29 June 1941. This was the last production model of the T-26 and had an improved turret and hull, of welded construction.

▲33

33. A BA-10 armoured car destroyed in Lvov, eastern Poland, on 25 June 1941. The BA-10 was the Soviet Army's standard armoured car, although predecessors like the BA-6 were still encountered in 1941.

34. A brand new T-34 Model 1941 knocked out near Jazow Stary in eastern Poland, 25 June 1941. This version, which was fitted with the new F-34 gun, had not yet been accepted for service use in June 1941, and was thus seen only in very small numbers.

35. A group of T-34 Model 1940s of the 4th Mechanized Corps disabled during fighting along the Jaworow–Lvov road, 30 June 1941. This particular tank is from the 1941 production batch: it features the newer cast turret but the older L-11 gun.

36. A T-35 of the 34th Tank Division, photographed in the Ukraine in June 1941. About 40 of these tanks were in service with the 34th Tank Division, and most seem to have been abandoned in the fighting around Lvov owing to mechanical problems. (J. Grandsen)

37. A T-35 Model 1938 in the Ukraine in June 1941. This is a rare vehicle indeed – only six were built. (J. Grandsen)

38. Another view of the abandoned T-35 Model 1938 of the 34th Tank Division. (J. Grandsen)

▲34 ▼35

36▲

37▲ 38▼

39. A T-34 Model 1940, 34th Tank Division, again abandoned in the Ukraine in June 1941. This particular vehicle has the welded turret rather than the later cast turret.
40. The Soviet Army made pill-boxes from the turrets of old T-18 tanks.
41. The KV-2 Dreadnought was undoubtedly a great shock to German troops in June 1941. It was virtually invulnerable to any tank or anti-tank gun, and could only be stopped by heavy artillery or 88mm anti-aircraft guns. However, the Red Army lost most of its KV-2s to mechanical breakdowns, usually attributable to a defective clutch or transmission. This Model 1941 was knocked out in Lada on the Lepel–Lvov road on 6 July 1941.
42. A T-34 Model 1940 of the 4th Mechanized Corps abandoned in Lvov on 30 June 1941. The Model 1940 suffered from severe teething troubles with its transmission, and the crew of this tank went so far as to bring along an extra transmission unit, lashed to the rear engine deck.

41▲   42▼

23

▲43

▼44

▼45

43. Another view of the abandoned T-34 Model 1940 in Lvov, here being inspected by local children.

44. A BT-7 Model 1935 being used in its wheeled mode. This vehicle was also abandoned in Lvov in June 1941.

45. A French R-35 tank converted for use as a turretless artillery tractor passes a wrecked BA-10 in Lithuania, July 1941.

46. A KV-2 of the 4th Mechanized Corps captured by German forces in Lvov in June 1941. The 4th, commanded by A. A. Vlasov, was one of the best equipped of the Soviet mechanized corps, and had about 460 T-34s amongst its 860 tanks.

47. The most common air defence vehicle in the Soviet Army was the 4M, which consisted of a GAZ-AA truck fitted with a quad 7.62mm Maxim machine gun mounting. This 4M was knocked out during the heroic defence of the Brest fortress.

▲48

48. The most numerous variant of the T-26 was the Model 1933, which was in production from 1933 to 1937. This example came to grief in the outskirts of Wilno on 3 July 1941.

49. A Stalinets S-60 (a copy of the American Caterpillar design) abandoned south-west of Wilno with a 107mm gun Model 1910/30 in tow. The S-60 was one of the more common artillery tractors in Soviet service.

50. The 7th Panzer Division used captured French Panhard P.178 armoured cars in lieu of German types like the SdKfz 222. This particular P.178 was named 'Löwe' (Lion).

51. Another P.178 armoured car of the 7th Panzer Division in Lithuania in July 1941.

▼49

50▲   51▼

▲52

▲53　▼54

52. An SdKfz 251 Ausf A manages to free a P.178 from marshy soil by placing matting under its wheels.

53. A German cavalry patrol examines an abandoned OT-26 flame-thrower tank.

54. A German truck burns fiercely near the wrecks of a T-34 Model 1941 and an OT-133 following the Jucourica tank battle.

55. The burning remains of a Soviet column following an action with German tanks near Jucourica. In the foreground is a T-34 Model 1941.

56. One day after the Jucourica tank battle, a German truck column passes a wrecked T-34 Model 1941. This is a cast-turreted Model 1941, probably fresh off the assembly lines.

57. A pair of PzSpWg Panhard 178(f)s. These vehicles are unusual in that their guns have been removed. They were attached to the 7th Panzer Division.

▲ 58

58. The Germans modified a small number of P.178 armoured cars by installing additional radio gear and a large external frame antenna. These were designated PzSpWg Panhard 178-P.204(f).
59. Turrets from old T-26 and BT-5 tanks in use as makeshift pill-boxes along the Soviet frontier.
60. A PzKpfw IV and an SdKfz 254 wheel-cum-track scout vehicle of the 7th Panzer Division in Lithuania in July 1941. The Austrian-built SdKfz 254 was not a particularly common vehicle during this period.
61. German troops pass an abandoned OT-130 flamethrower tank. The elaborate red star insignia on the bow is most unusual.
62. One of the rarer Soviet flamethrower tank types was the T-134, some of which were armed with a 45mm gun. This one has only the flame projector. (J. Grandsen)

▲ 59   ▼ 60

▲63　▼64

63. A BT-7 knocked out in the outskirts of Wilno on 25 June 1941. This tank still has the 1940 Baltic invasion cross on the roof, as is evident by the slight overlap of this insignia on to the turret sides.
64. A cast-turreted T-34 Model 1940, knocked out in the outskirts of Wilno on 25 June 1941.
65. A good view of a T-34 Model 1940 destroyed in the fighting in the Ukraine in early July 1941. It has taken hits through the thinner rear armour.
66. The Hungarian Fast Corps which fought with allied German units in the Soviet Union in 1941 had 48 of these Csaba armoured cars in service at the outset of the campaign. (I. Bajtos)

66▼

▲67 ▼68

67. An SdKfz 251 Ausf A armoured staff halftrack of the 7th Panzer Division in Lithuania in June 1941.
68. An SdKfz 263 communications armoured car passes through Wilno after the capture of the city by the 7th Panzer Division.

69. A column of PzKpfw 38(t) Ausf Es passes through Wilno on 3 July 1941.
70. A PzKpfw IV Ausf D parades through Wilno on 3 July 1941 after the successful battles to cross the Nieman river.

70▼

71. The victories over the Red Army were not without their costs, as is evident from this photograph of a PzKpfw III Ausf G which was heavily shot up by Soviet tanks during the fighting around Borisov on 3 July 1941.

72. The Soviet Army left a small rearguard at the Berezina river bridge at Smolensk to protect the demolition teams. It was overrun before the bridge could be destroyed. Air protection was being offered by this 4M quad Maxim air defence truck, which was thoroughly mauled in the attempt to hold the bridge.

73. A gutted BT-7 Model 1937 sits in mute testimony to the ferocity of the fight for the Berezina river bridge at Smolensk. To the left is an SdKfz 10/4 with 2cm AA gun.

74. An SdKfz 263 southwest of Lepel, 4 July 1941. German tactics were heavily dependent on the success of communications vehicles like these in co-ordinating the actions of tank subunits.

75. This KV-1 Model 1940 shows quite clearly why the Germans so feared this tank: at least three solid hits are evident on the turret, without penetration. The tank was finally knocked out at Zelva, 33km west of Slonim, on 7 July 1941.

73 ▲

74 ▲   75 ▼

▲76   ▼77

78▲

76. A German soldier inspects an abandoned OT-26. The long flame projector is clearly visible.
77. A factory-fresh T-34 Model 1941 lies abandoned at the edge of a river after the battle at Zelva, 7 July 1941.
78. One of the oddest armoured cars in German service in 1941 was this vehicle named 'Jaguar'. Seemingly a captured Russian BA-10, it in fact appears to be a Spanish-built BA-6 copy produced during the Spanish Civil War and later purchased by the Germans, presumably to serve with a Brandenburger unit to infiltrate Soviet positions. It was later captured by Soviet forces. (J. Grandsen)
79. A BA-10 knocked out while retreating. The device strapped around the rear hull of this armoured car is supplementary track which could be placed over the rear wheels of the vehicle to convert it into a halftrack.

79▼

80. A Komsomolets Model 1937 artillery tractor near Butovice, 7 July 1941. The vehicle may have been abandoned owing to mechanical problems as the rear seats have been folded down for better access to the rear-mounted engine.

81. A T-26 Model 1937 disabled during the battle at Senno on 10 July 1941. The T-26 was the most common type of tank in Russian service in 1941, with about 11,000 on the inventory.

82. The Hungarian Fast Corps deployed 81 of these Toldi light tanks in action in 1941 when it invaded the USSR. The Toldi was a licence-built version of the Swedish Landsverk L-60.

83. Just before the outbreak of the war, 400 old T-18 tanks were rebuilt as T-18M light tanks and issued to infantry units in the western USSR; the remaining 560 T-18s were mostly dug in as pillboxes, as shown in an earlier photograph. (J. Grandsen)

80▶

▼81

82▲   83▼

▲84

84. German troops inspect a T-37 amphibious tank abandoned by the roadside. This particular T-37 is from a late production batch and is fitted with the larger, welded turret.

85. A French UE artillery tractor in German service rests in the shade in Dunaburg, Latvia, 11 July 1941. This light armoured tractor was used mainly for towing light anti-tank guns.

86. A factory-fresh T-34 Model 1941 abandoned in a town square. This is a new production machine, witness the newer, cast turret.

87. A pair of burnt-out BT-2s in a street in Vitebsk on 12 July 1941 after German tanks have passed through.

88. A Komsomolets lies abandoned outside the Vitebsk Polytechnic. This is the later production version of the Komsomolets with the enlarged machine gun position.

▼85

▲89

89. A T-34 Model 1940 and Model 1941 abandoned after having been bogged down in the Tolotshchin marsh near the Drut river, 80km east of Borisov, on 14 July 1941.

90. The most heavily armoured version of the KV series was the KV-1E, an example of which is seen here by the roadside near Gauri, Latvia, on 14 July 1941. The clutches in these early KVs were often so troublesome that third and fourth gear could not be engaged, reducing road speed to a crawl.

91. A PzKpfw II of the 17th Panzer Division after the fighting at Tolotshchin on 14 July 1941. The prominent 'G' insignia was adopted by tanks under General Heinz Guderian's command.

▲90 ▼91

92. A StuG III Ausf C or D in action in July 1941. These vehicles were used to provide direct fire support for infantry units, and would play an increasingly important role on the Eastern Front.
93. A Komintern artillery tractor, knocked out near Malhava, Latvia, on 14 July 1941. It is towing a 76mm anti-aircraft gun.
94. A StuG III assault gun firing on Russian positions during the July 1941 fighting.

92▲

93▲   94▼

▲95   ▼96

95. The Slovak Fast Corps in Russia was equipped with Czechoslovak Army equipment such as this LT-35 – better known to the Germans as the PzKpfw 35(t).

96. The T-26 Model 1937 was essentially similar to late-production T-26 Model 1933s but had a fully welded hull and a new turret with sloping sides.

97. One of the more unusual command cars in German service in 1941 was the Belgian Marmon-Herrington-Ford armoured tractor. This vehicle was photographed near Lukty outside Vitebsk on 15 July 1941.

98. The SdKfz 253 was an observation version of the SdKfz 250 scout armoured car and differed from that vehicle in having an armoured roof with a circular cupola instead of an open roof.

97▲   98▼

▲99   ▼100

99. A BT-7 Model 1935 and BT-8 knocked out during the fighting near Dulovka on 15 July 1941.

100. The PzKpfw II Ausf F Flamm was the standard German flamethrower tank in 1941. Three battalions entered Russia in 1941, but they were not particularly successful.

101. BA-10 armoured cars go into action in the late summer of 1941. Many BA-10s were transferred from the Far East in the summer of 1941 to reinforce the heavily depleted units in western Russia.

102. A PzKpfw IV Ausf D of the 20th Panzer Division leads a column of PzKpfw 38(t)s during the fighting on 22 July 1941.

101▲ 102▼

▲103 ▼104

103. A rearguard of a T-34 Model 1941 and a BT-7 Model 1937 lie abandoned somewhere in the Ukraine, July 1941. The BT-7 is unusual in that, by this time, most new-production tanks had whip antennas instead of the obsolete 'clothes-lines'.

104. A platoon of BA-10s in action in the summer of 1941.

105. A T-26 Model 1933 knocked out along the Smolensk–Jarzevo highway on 23 July 1941.

106. A StuG III Ausf C or D of StuG Brigade 203 in action in July 1941. The brigade's white elephant insignia is apparent on the superstructure.

107. A column of PzKpfw IIIs and SdKfz 250s advances towards a recently defeated Russian tank column. A burning BT-5 can be seen to the left. (J. Grandsen)

105 ▲

106 ▲   107 ▼

▲108

108. A T-38 amphibious tank knocked out by Hungarian troops in the Ukraine in 1941. (I. Bajtos)
109. A BT-8 captured by Hungarian forces during the fighting in the Ukraine in July 1941. (I. Bajtos)
110. A rare example of a BT-7A artillery tank. This vehicle had a

larger turret than the standard BT-7 tank, and was armed with a 76.2mm gun.
111. Another view of the BT-7A artillery tank, alongside a T-27 tankette captured by Hungarian forces in the Ukraine in 1941. (I. Bajtos)

▼109

110▲ 111▼

112. Officers of a T-26
tank battalion draw up
plans prior to an attack,
summer 1941. (J.
Grandsen)
113. T-28 medium tanks
launch an attack in the
summer of 1941. These
lumbering old vehicles
were seldom encoun-
tered after the August
1941 tank battles, most
having been lost by then.
(Sovfoto)
114. A German soldier
examines an abandoned
KV-1 Model 1940.
Notice the hit against the
thickly armoured gun
trunnion.

▲112

▲113 ▼114

115. A T-28 captured by Hungarian forces in the Ukraine in the summer of 1941 and used by them in the fighting. (I. Bajtos)

116. On 24 July 1941, the Germans surprised a train unloading tanks at Jarzevo railway station and wiped the unit out with very little cost.

117. A BA-20 light scout car lies abandoned near Zviahel in the Ukraine, 26 July 1941.

115▲

116▲ 117▼

▲118

▲119　▼120

118. This T-34 Model 1941 ended its days after stumbling into a bog near Mushchkotishchi on 1 August 1941.

119. A T-26 Model 1939 knocked out during the fighting at Opotschka, 4 August 1941.

120. A Panzerbefehls-wagen Ausf H command tank of the 14th Panzer Division during the advance on Krivoi-Rog in the Ukraine on 14 August 1941.

121. A KV-2 Model 1941 Dreadnought knocked out in the Ukraine on 26 August 1941. Only 334 KV-2s were produced, and most were lost in the summer 1941 fighting.

122. A StuG III Ausf C or D of StuG Brigade 286 during the August 1941 fighting.

▲123

123. A military policeman directs traffic, in this case a Voroshilovets artillery tractor, the heaviest such vehicle in Soviet service in 1941.
124. A T-38 amphibious tank captured by Finnish troops in the 1941 fighting.
125. A KV-1E heavy tank and a T-34 Model 1941 medium tank lie abandoned. (James Kitchens III)
126. LT-35 light tanks of the Slovak Fast Corps undergo repairs in the Ukraine, 13 July 1941. (S. Zaloga)

▼124

▲127 ▼128

127. A T-28E medium tank knocked out by Finnish troops at Praasa, September 1941. The T-28E was an up-armoured version of the T-28 Model 1938 and was produced as a result of the 1940 war. (Esa Muikku)

128. A BT-5 knocked out by Finnish forces during the fighting in Karelia in the autumn of 1941. The unit insignia is unusual for the period. (Esa Muikku)

129. Finnish troops take a rest next to a BT-5 Model 1934 tank knocked out at Saama-jarvi in September 1941. (Esa Muikku)

130. A column of Soviet armour, which includes a T-133, a T-28 and (foreground) a BT-7 Model 1937, knocked out by Finnish troops near Aunus in the autumn of 1941. (Esa Muikku)

129▲ 130▼

▲131 ▼132

131. A BT-7 Model 1937 disabled by the Finnish Army at Praasa in 1941. (Esa Muikku)

132. An OT-133 photographed during the summer of 1941. Although the front flame projector cannot be seen, this vehicle can be identified as a flame-thrower tank by the fact that the turret is offset to the right and by the feed pipe for the flame fuel cistern on the right-hand side of the rear of the hull.

133. An SdKfz 247 armoured command vehicle. This is a rare photograph, since the SdKfz 247 was issued only on the basis of one per scout battalion commander in each panzer division.

134. A PzKpfw III undergoes track repairs, 14 August 1941. (J. Grandsen)

135. A Panzerjäger I Ausf B passes a StuG III somewhere in Russia, September 1941. By this stage in the war the Ausf B was obsolete, and not able to deal with tanks like the T-34. (J. Grandsen)

133▲

134▲   135▼

136. A pair of T-27 tankettes captured by Hungarian forces. These obsolete vehicles were used for scouting by Soviet infantry units, some of which also converted them into unarmed artillery tractors or ammunition supply vehicles. (I. Bajtos)

137. A PzKpfw III Ausf J of the 2nd Panzer Division fords a small stream. (J. Grandsen)

138. A group of T-40 amphibious tanks carries a Soviet infantry unit into combat in the autumn of 1941.

▲136

▲137 ▼138